Votes for W

Contents

Written by Jane Bingham

Collins

The right to vote

In most parts of the world today, women have the **right** to vote.
But women have not always had this right.

If you vote in an **election**, you can make a difference to how your country is run.

A hundred years ago, most women were not allowed to vote.

All over the world, women had to fight for voting rights.

This is the story of how women won the right to vote.

Kept at home

In the nineteeth century, women had very little freedom. Girls often got married before they were 20 years old.

Most men did not want women to have their own ideas.

Many people thought that women should not take part in life outside the home. But some brave women dared to be different. They believed that women should have the right to vote.

Nineteenth-century women had to **obey** their husbands.

Change begins

In the 1860s, the women's suffrage **movement** began. Suffrage means the right to vote. People who **campaign** for the right to vote are called suffragists.

The suffragists in New Zealand had a very successful campaign. In 1893, New Zealand became the first country to allow women to vote.

Suffragists campaigned in many countries. These American suffragists were on a **protest** march in New York in 1912.

Women's suffrage in Britain

The suffragists in Britain fought a long and difficult campaign. Sometimes they went on protest marches. Sometimes they held meetings to spread their ideas.

This large meeting was held in Hyde Park in London in 1913.

Suffragists from the north of England demonstrated in London in 1910.

In 1897, the National Union of Women's Suffrage Societies (NUWSS) was started in Britain. Millicent Fawcett was the leader of the NUWSS. She believed in the power of peaceful protests. The NUWSS tried to put pressure on the British **government**. But the government still refused to allow women to vote.

Millicent Fawcett

9

A stronger campaign

In 1903, a new campaign group was formed in Britain. It was called the Women's Social and Political Union (WSPU). The WSPU was led by Emmeline Pankhurst and her daughters, Christabel and Sylvia.

Emmeline, Christabel and Sylvia Pankhurst

Members of the WSPU wanted to force the government to change the voting laws. They were even prepared to use violent methods. Violent campaigners were called suffragettes. Some of them smashed windows and set fire to buildings.

Some suffragettes smashed shop windows.

Some suffragettes chained themselves to iron railings and refused to move to make sure their protest was noticed.

Violence and hunger strikes

Suffragettes who broke the law were **arrested** and sent to prison.

Emmeline Pankhurst being arrested in 1914

Once they were in prison, some suffragettes went on hunger strike. They refused to eat as a protest against the government.

Some of the hunger strikers became so weak that they had to be released from prison. They were taken to hospital or sent home to recover.

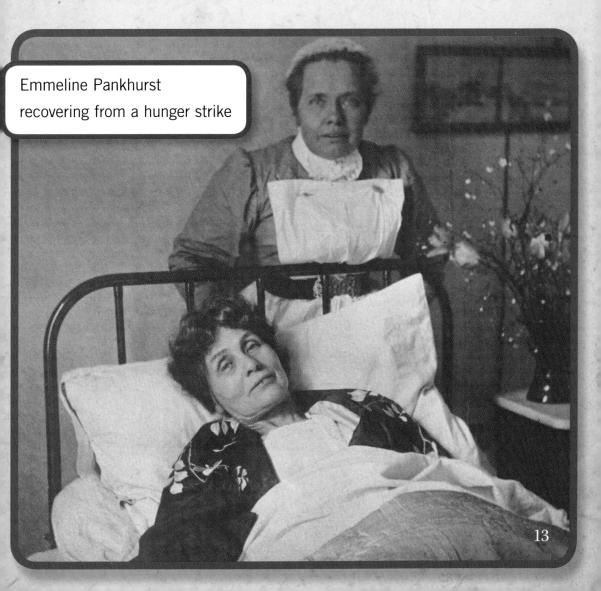

Emmeline Pankhurst recovering from a hunger strike

"Cat and mouse"

In 1913, the British government made a new law. The law said that when hunger strikers fell ill, they should be released from prison. But when the strikers were strong again, they should be sent back to prison.

People called this law the "Cat and Mouse Act". They said the government was like a cat that lets a mouse escape, but then catches it again.

Many people thought the government was being very cruel to suffragettes. They were shocked when they found out that some of the strikers were forced to eat and drink.

The government was shown as a cruel cat that was very unkind to the suffragettes.

TORTURING WOMEN IN PRISON

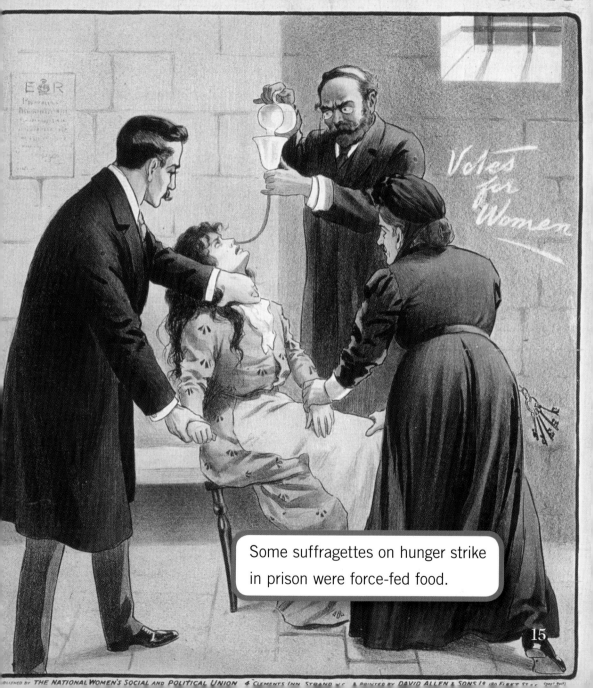

Some suffragettes on hunger strike in prison were force-fed food.

PUBLISHED BY THE NATIONAL WOMEN'S SOCIAL AND POLITICAL UNION 4 CLEMENTS INN STRAND W.C & PRINTED BY DAVID ALLEN & SONS L.D 180 FLEET ST.E.C

Anti-suffragists

Some British women hated the suffragists. In 1908, Mrs Humphrey Ward started the Women's National Anti-Suffrage League.

members of the Anti-Suffrage League

The anti-suffragists said that women should stay at home. They believed that only men should vote. They said that men did all the important jobs, so men should decide how the country was run.

EVERYBODY
WORKS BUT
MOTHER:
SHE'S A
SUFFRAGETT

This anti-suffrage cartoon suggested that women were trying to be more powerful than men.

I WANT TO VOTE, BUT
MY · WIFE · WONT · LET · ME

17

War and change

In 1914, World War I began. The war led to many changes. When the men went away to fight, women took over their jobs.

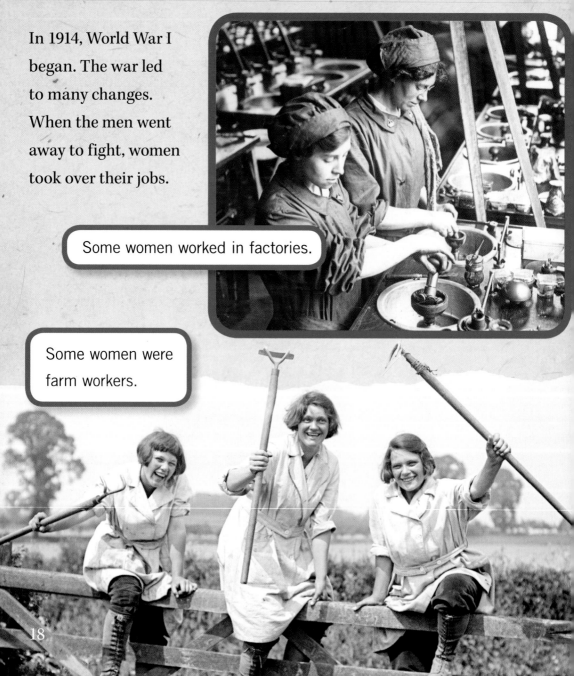

Some women worked in factories.

Some women were farm workers.

Some brave women worked as nurses on the battlefields.

By the end of the war in 1918, it was clear that women's lives were changing. Many people thought that women now deserved the right to vote.

The fight is won

In 1918, British women over the age of 30 won the right to vote. Ten years later, all British women over 21 were allowed to vote. In the 1920s, many other countries gave women the right to vote. Today, almost all countries in the world allow women to vote.

This woman was voting for the first time in Britain.

American women won the right to vote in 1920.

Glossary

arrested	taken by the police for breaking the law
campaign	to take part in actions to spread a message or ask for change
election	voting to choose a leader
government	a group of people elected to run a country
movement	a group of people with shared ideas working together
obey	to do what someone else decides or teaches
protest	to show disagreement with something, often in large crowds
right	agreement in law

Index

How women got the vote

1860s
Women's suffrage began.

1893
New Zealand was the first country to allow women to vote.

1860   1870   1880   1890

1897
National Union of Women's Suffrage Societies was started in Britain.

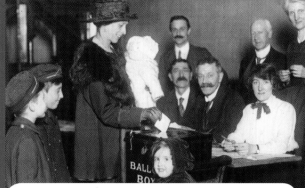

1903

Women's Social and Political Union was formed in Britain and was led by Emmeline Pankhurst and her daughters Christabel and Sylvia.

1918

World War I ended and women in Britain over 30 were given the right to vote.

1928

Women in Britain over 21 were allowed to vote.

1900   1910   1920   1930

1914

World War I began and women took over men's jobs.

1920

Women in the USA won the right to vote.

23

Ideas for reading

Written by Gillian Howell
Primary Literacy Consultant

Learning objectives: *(reading objectives correspond with Gold band; all other objectives correspond with Ruby band)* read independently and with increasing fluency longer and less familiar texts; know how to tackle unfamiliar words that are not completely decodable; identify and summarise evidence from a text to support a hypothesis

Curriculum links: History, Citizenship

Interest words: campaign, violence, election, century, suffrage, societies, pressure, social, national, league

Resources: pens, paper, cardboard, paints

Word count: 762

Getting started

- Read the title and discuss the cover photo. Ask the children to describe who is in the photo and what is happening.

- Ask what the children think the book will be about. Turn to the back cover, read the blurb together and check if their predictions were correct. Discuss what *vote* means and why women wanted the right to vote.

- Turn to the contents page and read the list of section headings. If children struggle with *suffrage* and *campaign*, ask them to look for the smaller words within each one, e.g. *rage* and *camp*. Explain that the *g* in *campaign* is silent.

Reading and responding

- Ask the children to read to p5 and point out the captions. Ensure that they read the captions as they continue to gain further information from them.

- Ask the children if their original ideas about why women wanted the vote have changed and why. Ask the children to read to the end of the book and to find out and make notes of three things women did to try to gain the right to vote.